'My Polish Teacher's Tie' by Helen Dunmore:

the Study Guide

Natalie Twigg

ISBN: 978-1494279455

Table of Contents

Author

Helen Dunmore was born in 1952 in Yorkshire. She was the second of four children and her father was the eldest of twelve; she attributes being part of a large family as instrumental to her prolific writing career. Amongst her various credentials she won the inaugural Orange Prize for Fiction in 1996, a prize awarded specifically to female writers, with her third novel *A Spell of Winter*.

'My Polish Teacher's Tie' is one of 18 short stories extracted from her book *Ice Cream. Ice Cream* was also nominated for the Orange Prize in 2003.

The author's recurrent themes consist of love and loss, food and landscapes.

Plot

'My Polish Teacher's Tie' is set in a school canteen and its protagonist (the leading character) is a school dinner lady, Carla Carter. It is written in the first person. In the fourth paragraph Carla reveals that she is half Polish, although she does not speak the language. Her English father objected to Carla speaking Polish with her mother, believing that it would confuse his child.

At the weekly staff meeting the Head announces plans to arrange a teacher exchange. We are told that several Polish teachers are looking for pen friends in English schools (to improve their written English). Carla volunteers and begins corresponding with Stefan, or Steve as he prefers to be known. Carla harbours a nagging guilt, knowing that Steve believes he is communicating with another teacher, not a school dinner lady.

Through their correspondence Carla's love of poetry is rekindled and her hunger to learn more of her Polish heritage exposed. Steve's letters provide her with a great source of pleasure and the frequency of their exchanges begins to increase.

After what we can assume have been several weeks the Head announces that a teacher will be visiting from Poland on exchange. That teacher is Steve. Carla is mortified, knowing that Steve will discover her real identity. Their correspondence ceases after Carla receives a letter from Steve, confirming his exchange visit. She thinks the tone is polite but cooler and she concludes that Steve feels rejected, having assumed her to be a teacher and aware of his imminent arrival, but having not volunteered to play host. She considers her options, including taking time off sick, but eventually persuades herself to stop worrying.

After Steve's arrival at the school and before Carla has met him she overhears a conversation between two teachers. Valerie Kenwood, who is playing host to Steve, speaks of him in a disparaging manner, criticizing his accent, his clothes (particularly his ties) and his preoccupation with literature. Carla then spots Steve in the canteen and summons up the courage to approach him, despite her feelings of guilt and inadequacy.

Steve, who is delighted to meet Carla contrary to her expectations, breaks into song. It is a song that Carla finally recognises from her early childhood. The story closes with the two of them singing in faltering duet much to the surprise of the Head.

Characters

Carla Carter

Although not mentioned in the story, we can assume from the omissions that Carla is a single parent, mother to only-child Jade. She describes herself in the first paragraph as "part-time catering staff, that's me £3.89 per hour." She is someone who is focused on her perceived standing in society and refers to herself continually in a self-deprecating fashion. Carla is a quiet woman but acutely conscious of her surroundings and her inner-monologue demonstrates a highly observant and empathetic nature. On occasions she can be sarcastic, scathing and quite child-like.

Stefan (Steve) Jeziorny

Steve is a polite young Polish teacher with a passion for literature and poetry. He is someone who enjoys sharing his passion as indicated by the contents of his letters to Carla. He is portrayed as a driven man with a humorous and optimistic outlook on life.

The scenes in the canteen reveal that he is not a judgemental person and that he too lacks confidence and self-esteem.

The Head

The Head is presented through Carla's narrative as a bumbling man, lacking in sincerity and with little knowledge of his staff outside the teaching fraternity.

Valerie Kenward

Valerie, Steve's host and a teacher at the school, is portrayed as a smug, greedy, highly critical woman, lacking in empathy. Her children appear to have inherited some of her worst traits. She is not someone to reason with and voices her opinions in a bullish way. Both she and the Head represent the anti-hero to the characters of Carla and Steve.

Language

The language used throughout the story is simple and colloquial. Sentences are short and contractions used throughout: "Somebod_y'd_ remember me...." This gives the story a very chatty and intimate feel. Steve's language, meanwhile, demonstrates that whilst his English is highly competent, it lacks the fluidity of native speakers: "You will know from your school, Carla, that I will come to England". Whilst it makes perfect grammatical sense, we would write: "that I will <u>be</u> com<u>ing</u> to England".

Carla's use of language changes dramatically on meeting Steve. She begins to introduce similes: "He was tense as a guitar string" and "It went through me like a knife through butter". She also uses alliteration: "His big bright tie blazing".

The use of these poetic devices suggests an awakening in Carla, a determination to put aside her sense of inadequacy and to embrace her love of poetry.

Themes

Taken at its most literal and simplistic level, 'My Polish Teacher's Tie' describes how a school dinner lady rises above her personal inadequacies to explore her past and broaden her horizons. Steve provides the role of catalyst. A kind of alchemy ensues, arising from the collision of two worlds.

Sense of Self-worth

The theme of self-worth runs through the core of the story. Carla's self-worth or, rather, lack of it, is demonstrated by her acute awareness of her perceived social standing. In line 100 she identifies herself as being a separate entity from the teaching staff: "Colleagues don't wear blue overalls and white caps and work for £3.89 an hour". Similarly, on line 25 Carla recounts how "the meeting broke up and the Head vanished in a knot of teachers...." The use of the word "knot" in describing the collective of teachers again suggests that Carla perceives herself as an outsider and that the collective, the "knot", is impenetrable. In line 27 she observes that 'teachers are used to getting out of the way of catering staff without really seeing them'. She feels invisible.

Her opinions on the teaching staff are made clear by her omission in the opening paragraph: "I dish out tea and buns to the teachers twice a day, and I shovel chips on the kids' trays at dinner-time. It's not a bad job. I like the kids". She 'likes' the kids but makes no such comment on the teachers.

In line 22 she takes ownership of her lesser role: "I wrung out a cloth and wiped my surfaces", as if to say 'I know my place'. And in line 29, in trying to get the Head's attention she repeats "excuse me" three times, which serves to stress her invisibility. When the Head finally notices Carla, she recounts how he "stitched a smile on his face", suggesting that Carla finds him insincere and reluctant to engage with her. He then stumbles over her name and assumes that whatever she wants it means trouble: "Oh, er - Mrs, er – Carter. Is there a problem?" The hesitation in identifying Carla by name acts to highlight her sense of inferiority.

Similarly, in her relationship with Steve, she feels that without hanging on to the pretence of being a teacher he will become instantly disinterested, drawing her assumption from the attitude of the teaching staff around her. In line 106, having just been made aware of Steve's impending visit, she ruminates: "He'd think I was trying to make a fool of him, making him believe I was a teacher. Me, Carla Carter, part-time catering assistant, writing to him about poetry" (line 121-122).

Steve qualifies her interest in poetry; without him she feels unworthy to pursue her interest alone: "And then there was the poetry book I'd bought. It seemed a shame to bin it. It might come in use for Jade, I thought".

Loss and Retrieval of Identity

We learn that Carla is half-Polish very early on in the story. Her mother used to read rhymes to her, until her English father objected to her speaking Polish. She recounts her father's rationale in line 15: "You'll get her all mixed up, now she's going to school. What use is Polish ever going to be to her?" In line 13 she conveys how detached she feels from her Polish heritage: "I'm half-Polish. They don't know that here. My name's not Polish or anything...I spoke Polish till I was six, baby Polish...." Later in the paragraph she admits she recalls nothing of the language: "I can't speak it now. I've got a tape, a tape of me speaking Polish with Mum. I listen, and think I'm going to understand what we're saying, and then I don't".

Through her correspondence with Steve, she slowly retrieves some of her lost language and heritage but she also begins to identify herself as something beyond just a dinner lady. When they eventually meet in line 154 the layout of the dialogue breaks from convention: "'Hello', I said. He jumped up, held out his hand. 'How do you do?' he asked...'" Here both of them speak on the same line, which is entirely unique within the body of the story. Sharing the line evokes a sense of shared identity, a unification of two lonely souls.

The story closes with Steve breaking into song. It is a song that Carla recognises and she joins in. She is finally reunited with her past. With a renewed sense of self, she allows herself to be defined by who she is rather than what she does. The Head, astounded by the singing says: "Good heavens. How very remarkable. I didn't realise you were Polish, Mrs... er...". To which Carla replies: "Nor did I".

The sentence continues with Carla's inner monologue: 'But I wasn't going to waste time on the Head. I wanted to talk about poetry. I smiled at Steve'.

The Imperialist Legacy

Valerie Kenward's scathing attitude towards Steve and her outspoken ridicule of his accent, clothing and conversation are all suggestive of a deeply entrenched sense of British superiority. Carla describes how "the Head was wagging a sheaf of papers in front of him (Steve), talking very loudly, as if he were deaf". This again indicates that Steve is perceived to be a lesser being. The theme is also touched upon in line 15 where Carla's English father dismisses the value of the Polish language and perhaps his daughter: "What use is Polish going to be to her?" The contempt shown towards Poland and Steve himself could be attributed to imperialism's legacy – an unspoken but continuing sense of national supremacy and prejudice.

Hope

Steve's garish tie symbolises a beacon of hope, both for himself and Carla, it could be seen to represent a breaking down of prejudice and social judgement. Both find themselves on the receiving end of discrimination. A particularly good example for Carla is when she requests the Polish teacher's address in line 33 and the Head fails to see her as a potential pen friend: "'I was just wondering, could I have that address?' 'Address?' 'The Polish one. You said there was a Polish teacher who wanted an English penfriend.' 'Oh. Ah, yes.' He paused, looking at me as if it might be a trick question.'"

Valerie Kenward provides the voice of discrimination in Steve's case

Carla acknowledges Steve's slightly unusual appearance: "He was wearing a brown suit with padded shoulders. It looked too big for him. His tie was wider than normal ties, and it was red with bold green squiggles on it. It was a terribly <u>hopeful</u> tie". Notice how Carla herself associates the tie with hope.

The final paragraph is symbolic of the breaking down of prejudice, Steve has accepted Carla for what she is, not what she does and the tie becomes a metaphor for a world without discrimination, a world with hope:

His red tie with its bold green squiggles was much too wide and much too bright. It was a flag from another country, a better country than the ones either of us lived in 'I like your tie,' I said.

A Note on Ownership

The title of the book suggests that the protagonist is a school child. The first line of the story is also indicative of this: "I wear a uniform, blue overall and white cap with the school logo". However, we quickly learn that Carla is a school dinner lady. The use of "My" in the title suggests a sense of ownership. Later in the story Steve will address Carla with: "'Carla! You are Carla Carter. <u>My</u> penfriend.'" This language of ownership acts to highlight the bond between the two individuals who, aside from their own mutual relationship, appear lost and unconnected to any social grouping.

A Note on Steve's First Poem

The first poem Steve sends to Carla describes a bird in a coal mine. It becomes trapped but continues singing until it eventually dies. Everyone can hear it singing, but no one can find it. Traditionally canaries were used as a warning system for toxic levels of carbon monoxide and methane. If the bird died it gave the miners sufficient time to exit the mine before they too were poisoned. In a sense Steve could be seen to represent the bird he describes. He has three things in common with the creature, he is in a foreign environment, he feels lost and yet despite this in the final paragraphs he breaks into song. Steve, therefore, could be seen to represent Carla's canary, protecting her from her own poison – low self-esteem and a sense of not belonging.

Model Answers

In English and English Literature it is impossible to write a 'model' answer, because there are countless ways to write a good answer that will achieve a high grade. As a subject, English thrives on different opinions and individual insights – your own personal response. However, through teaching we come across a lot of students who say, "I have no idea how to start" or who have deep responses to a particular story but are unsure about how to put their ideas down on paper. So what follows are answers to questions asked by the exam board on the anthology in 2011 and 2012 – not perfect answers at all, but examples of what might have been written. If we have used words you do not understand, it is to encourage you to use them. There are some golden rules to remember when you write on literature: quote often but keep your quotations short and always comment on them; answer the question and use the words that the examiner uses in the question; do not write about the characters as if they are real people – they are not – they are imaginary creations of the writer; try to show an awareness of other interpretations – if something in a story is unclear or capable of being interpreted in more than one way, have the confidence to say so – provided you are answering the question.

The questions at Foundation and Higher Tier do differ in each examination session, and they also differ in that Foundation Tier questions use slightly simpler language and bullet points. We, however, make no distinctions below between the two tiers as the structure of the questions is essentially the same, as are the assessment objectives. We have kept the answers that follow to around one thousand words: they are not 'perfect' answers (such things do not exist in English Literature) and we could have written much more, but we are conscious that you have only a very limited amount of time to answer the question in the examination.

In the English Literature exam, as we are sure your teachers have told you, your work is being assessed against two separate assessment objectives (often called AOs). There are, in fact, four assessment objectives for English Literature, but only the first two are assessed on this exam paper.

Assessment Objective 1 requires you to:

respond to texts critically and imaginatively; select and evaluate textual detail to illustrate and support interpretations.

To address this assessment objective successfully, you need to show that you are aware that stories can be interpreted differently and you need to have a clear sense of how **you** respond critically to each story – Do you like it? Why? What is its overall effect? What is its tone, mood and atmosphere? You also need to refer to the text – "select... textual detail" – by using quotations and you have to "evaluate" the textual detail you select. In practice this means that every time you use a quotation, you should write a sentence after it which evaluates it – which explains why it is important or what its effect is. We would also advise you to keep your quotations as short and pithy as possible: after all, you have the text with you in the exam and you get no marks for copying out long parts of the story. And you have limited time – twenty minutes on each story, so you have to think and write quickly and effectively.

Assessment objective 2 requires you to:

explain how language, structure and form contribute to writers' presentation of ideas, themes and settings.

We are sure that you will have a good grasp of each story's themes, but note that this assessment objective asks you to focus on the ways language, form and structure contribute to the ways in which the ideas, themes and settings are brought out in the stories. You might feel a little puzzled about how to write about structure in a short story. (In poetry, by contrast, there is often a readily identifiable structure involving a rhyme scheme and stanzas or line length), but short stories also use structure, so elements like how a story begins and ends is a question of structure; flashbacks and changes of tense are part of structure; the order of events and the way writers choose to reveal some information slowly are parts of structure. Form too might be a question of when a writer reveals something to the reader – a piece of information that provides a twist or unexpected ending to the story.

On the exam paper you have a choice of two questions: you answer only one. Each question has two parts. Part (a) of each question will ask you to consider an aspect or a feature of a named story in the anthology, so you have no choice about which story to write about.

Part (b) will ask you to consider the same aspect or feature, but relating it to a story of your choice from the anthology. In our model answers we do the choosing in part (b) for you, but in the brief notes that follow each model answer, we do point out alternatives that might have been used. It is important that you choose for part (b) a story that works – given the demands of the question. Let's take one question as an example: part (a) might ask about Baines' use of symbolism in 'Compass and Torch'; part (b) will ask you to consider symbolism in another story: there is no right answer to this, but not every object in every story is symbolic, so you do have to think before you answer part (b) to make sure you are choosing a story that is appropriate and that will give you enough material to write about. On this exam paper there is no requirement for you to compare the two stories that you write about – you get no credit if you do so.

One final piece of advice: it is very important that you write roughly equal amounts on both stories, on both (a) and (b). In bold in the mark scheme that examiners use it states: "To achieve a mark in Band 3 or higher candidates should deal with both parts of the question. To achieve a mark in Band 6 candidates should offer a substantial treatment of both parts". Band 6 is the highest band. In the model answers that follow, we have tried to write roughly equal amounts on each part of each question. Make sure you leave yourself enough time to answer the second half of the question.

Question 1

Part (a) Write about how the opening of 'Anil' prepares the reader for the rest of the story

The opening of 'Anil' prepares us very well for some of the later events in the story. In the opening paragraph Noor tells us that the whole village was asleep apart from one little boy who was wide awake. Everyone in the village, Noor tells us, is dreaming, but their dreams are very ordinary: they "rarely amounted to anything" (lines 3 – 4). "Housewives dreamed of tomorrow's cooking and the children dreamed of waking up to another day, and the next, and the next, until it was over as soon as it began" (lines 5 – 7). Anil, however, is immediately established as different, not simply because he is awake, but why he is awake and the way that Noor describes it. He is staring through a hole in his parents' hut at a "small star which shone down upon him" (line 14). The fact that the star is shining on Anil is important because it suggests he is different, and this prepares us, generally, for his honesty about the murder he witnesses later and also for his departure at the end of the story to the city to gain an education. The star shining down on him suggests that he is special and destined for greater things. It also shows his sensitivity: Noor tells us "His parents would not stop to gape at a star" (line 18), but Anil did because he "believed in the magical wonders of life. Because his dreams were bigger than him" (lines 19 – 20), and this too prepares us both for his courage in telling the truth about what he has seen, but also his astonishing change of fortune at the end of the story.

The opening also establishes that Anil lives in a very poor village: there are many holes in the roof of his parents' hut. We are also told that Anil, although he does not know it, is destined to be the headman's servant – just as his father is now. Anil's mother is physically abused by his father: Anil can see the bruise on her shoulder where she has been hit the evening before when Anil's father came home drunk; this prepares us for the fact that women in this community are subject to violence – as we are to see with the murder and cover up of Marimuthu's wife.

Finally, Anil is also awake because his bladder is bursting and he desperately needs to go to the toilet. This reveals something important about his relationship with his parents: he does not want to wake his mother to ask to go out – because she is sleeping soundly and he is aware that his father has hit her, so Anil is established by Noor as kind and sympathetic. For the same reason, he dare not wake his father because to do so would be to risk his father's anger and the inevitable beating: "He decided that he did not need a walloping at this time of night" (line 40). This prepares us generally for the atmosphere of violence that the story contains. Because he is awake and decides to go outside on his own, Anil witnesses the murder which, together with his direct honesty, shapes the rest of the story.

Thus the opening of 'Anil' prepares us for Anil's being different and special in some way; it shows the poverty of the village and the status of women; and it gives a realistic reason for Anil to be up and about at that time of night. What we are not prepared for are the awful events that Anil witnesses and his dramatic departure at the end of the story – although the star shining down on him may, when we look back at the opening, hint at this.

Part (b) Write about how the opening of one other story from *Sunlight on the Grass* prepares the reader for the rest of the story

The first sentence of 'My Polish Teacher's Tie' reads: "I wear a uniform, blue overall and white cap with the school logo on it", in conjunction with the title itself and its possessive pronoun "my", we are initially lead to believe that the protagonist is a school pupil, when, in fact, she is a dinner lady. This is significant because one of the dominant themes in 'My Polish Teacher's Tie' is that of preconceptions and prejudice. Dunmore, effectively, tricks the reader into starting the story with their own preconceptions or assumptions which she then dismantles in the second sentence: "Part-time catering staff, that's me, £3.89 per hour". We now know that Carla is, in fact, a school dinner lady.

The protagonist then describes how she "dishes out tea and buns to the teachers twice a day" and "shovel chips on the kids' trays at dinner-time". Dunmore keeps the description of Carla's work here very simple, she does not 'serve' the children she 'shovels' chips; she is part time and on a meagre wage. The reader is left with low expectations of the protagonist from the outset and the author presents a woman with a self-deprecating nature, someone who is acutely aware of her social standing. This is highlighted in line 22 and 23 where the protagonist takes ownership of the humble objects of her work: "I wrung out a cloth and wiped my surfaces". The writer is indicating that the protagonist firmly knows her place.

Carla's obvious sense of not belonging on the staff is demonstrated in line 9 the Head "sees his staff together for ten minutes once a week...". The language Dunmore uses suggests that Carla is not part of the staff and in fact feels no affiliation with them. In line 3 the omission is pertinent: "It's not a bad job. I like the kids". The protagonist suggests by omission that she does not like the staff and at line 27 her sense of inferiority and lowliness is reiterated: "Teachers are used to getting out of the way of catering staff without really seeing them". Dunmore suggests here that Carla feels invisible, excluded, which is highlighted again in line 25 when "The meeting broke up and the head vanished in a knot of teachers...." Again the collective term 'knot' suggests a sense of exclusion or inferiority; it is something which she needs to penetrate in order to reach the Head.

Having summoned up the courage to approach the Head he "stitches a nice smile on his face"; the lack of spontaneity in his response and his forced smile suggest a lack of sincerity or genuine interest. He then stumbles over the protagonist's name (line 32): "Oh, er – Mrs, er – Carter...". Having expressed an interest in the pen-friend arrangement, the Head pauses "looking at me as if it might be a trick question..." These elements again support the theme of prejudice and preconceptions which the story goes on to explore.

Returning to lines 22 and 23: "I wrung out a cloth and wiped my surfaces" - this line is highly significant because of its relationship with the title. Both the surface and the Polish Teacher are claimed by the possessive pronoun 'my', which creates interest and a compulsion to read on to discover why the lowly protagonist feels able to make a personal claim on the teacher. The readers are steered towards surmising that a relationship will evolve between the two, but the author leaves us questioning, so we have to read on to find out.

Note

With this sort of question any story from the Anthology might have been used for part (b), because in a way every story's opening prepares you in some way for what is to follow, even if the writer withholds some information. A very good choice would have been 'Something Old, Something New' because the very first paragraphs contain the man's arrival in the Sudan and his mixed reaction to being abroad as well as the meeting of the lovers at the airport, where they cannot kiss each other, and where their behaviour is inhibited by the presence of her brother as well as cultural norms. Aboulela keeps returning to these preoccupations: the Scotsman continues to feel attracted and repelled by the Sudan, and their love is circumscribed by Muslim tradition: they are never alone until after the marriage.

But others would work equally well: line 20 of 'When the Wasps Drowned' reads - 'That was the day they dug up Mr Mordechai's garden' - which is actually an event that occurs only after the end of the story and which cryptically foreshadows the whole story, while arousing the reader's interest. With 'My Polish Teacher's Tie' the simplicity of the opening paradoxically does not prepare us especially well for the complex issues of identity that the story raises. Similarly, in 'The Darkness Out There' the pleasant and innocent opening can be seen as an effective contrast with the dark events that come to light as the story progresses.

Question 2

Part (a) Write about how Dunmore presents Carla, the narrator, in 'My Polish Teacher's Tie

Carla is presented as someone acutely aware of her self-perceived social standing and her position in staff hierarchy. In the first paragraph the protagonist describes herself purely in terms of her working position and she does this with emphasis on all the more negative traits of her role: her lowly wage, the part time nature of her position, even through to the language she uses to describe serving food : "Part-time catering staff, that's me, £3.89 per hour. I dish out tea and buns to the teachers twice a day and shovel chips on to the kids' trays at dinner-time." The choice of 'shovel' and 'dish' rather than 'serve' stresses that this is not a high-end catering establishment, merely a perfunctory school canteen.

Carla recognises herself as an entirely separate entity to the teaching staff. Dunmore describes how the dinner lady "wipe(s) my surfaces" (line23), the possessive 'my' suggests that she accepts her lesser role and at line 100 the protagonist explicitly states her position: "Colleagues don't wear blue overalls and white caps and work for £3.89 an hour." Carla is presented as someone who, while mindful of her position, has a propensity, through her inadequacies, to collectivise and dismiss the teaching staff. She generalises in line 27: "Teachers are used to getting out of the way of catering staff without really seeing them."

Having established that Carla recognises herself as a separate and lesser entity to the teachers, line 8 betrays a more sarcastic side to the protagonist. In divulging the teachers' kitty for entitlement to tea and buns, she says: "...Very keen on fairness, we are, here." It is clear that she does not consider herself part of the 'we' she describes and herein lies the sarcasm.

We learn through the story that Carla is a parent, probably a single parent. No reference is made to a partner or husband, but at times her rationale appears child-like. In line 53 she belligerently states: "I didn't write anything about my job. Let him think what he wanted to think. I wasn't lying". Similarly, in line 62 Dunmore has the protagonist confess that: "I used to write a bit every day then make myself wait until the middle of the week to send it." Both echo a child-like mentality.

Despite this Dunmore also presents Carla as an accurate but silent observer of human traits (line 78): "...said the head raising his voice the way he does so that one minute he's talking to you and the next it's a public announcement." Again, at line 117 Dunmore highlights how Carla is acutely way of the mannerisms of those around her: "...Always holding up the queue saying she's on a diet, and then taking the biggest bun." After she sees Steve, this observational side of her takes on an empathetic slant. Dunmore writes (line 142): "He was sitting stiffly upright, smiling in the way people smile when they don't quite understand what's going on" (line 142). She continues: "The Head was wagging a sheaf of papers in front of him, and talking very loudly as if he was deaf."

Finally, after having plucked up the courage to introduce herself to Steve, the protagonist is shown to embrace her love of poetry and language which, without Steve, she feels unable to embrace as demonstrated at line 121: "And then there was the poetry book I'd bought. It seemed a shame to bin it. It might come in use for Jade. I thought." Having met Steve, Dunmore introduces metaphor and analogy into Carla's language (line 156): "Tense as a guitar string" and (line 165): "It went through me like a knife through butter" (line 165). Finally, the protagonist concludes with a fresh confidence: "His red tie with its bold green squiggles was much too wide and much too bright. It was a flag from another country, a better country than the ones either of us lived in." Her final observations suggest a much richer and more sentient character than the story originally reveals.

Part (b) How does the writer present the narrator of one other story from *Sunlight on the Grass*?

The narrator of 'On Seeing the 100% Perfect Girl One Beautiful Spring Morning' is presented in an interesting way, because we know so little about him, even though Murakami uses him as the narrator, and because the story he tells is so unusual and rather timeless – it has elements reminiscent of fairy tales, but is set in modern Tokyo, with references to the very popular Harajuki district. His tone as narrator is at once self-deprecatory and very serious, so his story veers between poking fun at himself and how ridiculous he is, and a rather touching romantic yearning to fall in love with the 100% perfect girl of the title. He seems to believe in the possibility of perfect love, while at the same time mocking himself for doing so, for keeping faith in a romantic, optimistic view of relationships. This tension between his ideal and the down-to-earth reality of his life makes the story funny – in a very gentle, wistful, slightly melancholic way.

The narrator establishes a close relationship with the reader by directly addressing us, by using the present tense, which gives an immediacy to his style, and by the honesty of what he tells us. Having told us that he has seen the 100% perfect girl he admits "tell you the truth, she's not that good looking. She doesn't stand out in any way" (line 3). However he asserts that "I know from 50 yards away: she is the 100% perfect girl for me" (line 6). This slightly ridiculous scenario suggests that the narrator is very lonely and is desperate to meet the 100% perfect girl. He admits to the reader:

maybe you have your own particular favourite type of girl – one with slim ankles, say, or big eyes, or graceful fingers, or you're drawn for no good reason to girls who take their time with every meal (lines 9 – 12).

This is amusing because some of these characteristics are so random and so trivial that they seem a poor foundation for a lasting relationship. The narrator admits that "sometimes in a restaurant I catch myself staring at the girl at the table next to mine because I like the shape of her nose" (lines 12 – 13), but he admits as far as the 100% perfect girl he has seen: "I can't recall the shape of hers – or even if she had one" (line15). This brief image of a possibly nose-less woman is amusing and weird.

Of course, it would be even more weird to address a complete stranger on the street and the way he imagines the different things that he might have said to her is doubly amusing, because in the event he says nothing and when he turns to look at her she is lost in the crowd. It is clear that the narrator is partly living in a dream world: "Wish I could talk to her. Half an hour would be plenty" (line 28). As she gets closer he becomes more anxious: "How can I approach her? What should I say?" (line 37). He rejects the idea of asking her to spend half an hour for a conversation or asking her whether she knows if there are any all-night cleaners in the area: he dismisses these ideas as ridiculous. He considers telling her the simple truth: "Good morning. You are the 100% perfect girl for me" (lines 45 – 46). Interestingly he doesn't do this, not because it would be ridiculous or weird to say this to a complete stranger, so he says, but in case she rejects him.

The story that he then tells, which begins "Once upon a time there lived a boy and a girl" (line 64), is, he decides, what he should have said to the 100% perfect girl that he saw at random on the street. The story itself is about how he and the 100% perfect girl met and fell in love when they were younger, but how as the years passed and adulthood and maturity dominated their lives, they forgot about one another and, although they become "truly upstanding citizens who knew how to transfer from one subway line to another, who were fully capable of sending a special delivery letter at the post office" (lines 100 – 102), they lose the ability to love 100% and when they do pass each other on the street (as they have done at the start of Murakami's story), "the glow of their memories was far too weak, and their thoughts no longer had the clarity of fourteen years earlier" (lines 113 – 114). Without a word, they passed each other, disappearing into the crowd for ever.

The narrator of this story is a lonely 32-year-old man who yearns to rediscover the innocence and passion of youth and who perhaps naïvely believes, against all the odds, that somewhere for him is the 100% perfect girl. At the end of his fantasy story, he declares "Yes that's it, that is what I should have said to her" (line 117): as if this romantic but sad story, told to a complete stranger, would have been any less ridiculous than asking the whereabouts of an all-night cleaners.

Note

The other story that could have been used for part (b) is 'When the Wasps Drowned', because of the calm way Eveline describes the horrific events of that long, hot summer. The fact that her calmness might also be seen as a deliberate attempt not to think about all the things in her life that are changing would have given you a lot to write about. The same could be said for the matter-of-fact way in which the killing of the wasps is described. Another good focus would have been on the behaviour of Mrs Rutter and/or Sandra in 'The Darkness Out There', focusing on what they say and do. Lively also presents Mrs Rutter in an interesting way, and she uses structure and language to contrast how Mrs Rutter is now compared with how she was in the past.

Question 3

Answer **part (a)** and **part (b)**

Part (a)

How does the writer present feelings in 'On Seeing the 100% Perfect Girl One Beautiful April Morning'?

One of the most important things to notice about the presentation of feelings in this story is that they are completely central: indeed, the young man who narrates the story tells us only about his feelings for the perfect girl that he passed in the streets that morning. We know nothing about his work, his living arrangements, his hobbies and pastimes, or even his name – the entire story is focused on the feelings that he has about the perfect girl and the thoughts that she provokes.

In the opening of the story, which is written in the present tense to give it more immediacy and in which the narrator addresses the reader very casually in a matey, blokey way, the feelings that he has are clearly motivated by sexual attraction – although with a clear emphasis on fantasy or day-dreaming. He imagines that once he has spoken to her, 'we'd have lunch somewhere, maybe see a Woody Allen movie, stop by a hotel bar for cocktails. With any kind of luck, we might end up in bed' (lines 33 – 34). So he is clearly motivated by sexual desire. However, because he cannot think of any way of starting a conversation which will not be seen as ridiculous, his brief daydream is irrelevant: they pass without exchanging a word and soon she is lost in the crowd. It is clear that the narrator is disturbed and anxious because he can think of no way to start a conversation: 'In fact, even from fifty yards away she provokes 'a rumbling in my chest, and my mouth is as dry as a desert' (lines 7 – 8).

Prior to this, in conversation with a vague 'someone' (line 17) and in his remarks to the reader, the narrator has placed great emphasis on the qualities that might be a part of someone's 'perfect girl' and all the characteristics mentioned are physical ones: 'slim ankles', 'big eyes', 'graceful fingers', 'the shape of her eyes or the size of her breasts'. This concentration on the purely physical aspects of a woman's appearance may be typical of some men and can be quite offensive to women, since it pays no attention to their personality or character: it turns women into objects of male desire. In the first two pages of the story the only things which make this more than a day-dream of lust are his description of her as the 100% perfect girl, his anxiety about speaking to her and his amused self-awareness that even if he says, 'Good morning. You are the 100% perfect girl for me' (lines 45 – 46), she might well reply, 'Sorry… but you're not the 100% perfect boy for me' (lines 48 -49). The first two sides have a comic feel: there is the parody of male attitudes to women – reducing them to 'thin ankles'; the ridiculous idea of being able to tell that a woman is the 100% perfect girl from fifty yards away; even the idea of approaching a complete stranger on the street to tell her she is the 100% perfect girl. So we can say the feelings are not presented seriously by Murakami: he even allows the narrator an awareness of how ridiculous he is being.

The narrator then proceeds to tell us what he should have said to the girl he passed in the street, and he then launches into a version of how his life and the girl's might have been different had they met earlier in life and the feelings – while still retaining a strong element of fantasy – become much more serious in their presentation, because Murakami is making a serious point about what happens as we grow older and lose our youthful innocence.

The change in the story is marked by a change to the past tense and Murakami begins with the words 'Once upon a time' (line 64) which makes what follows have a fairy tale element. The pair meet and speak honestly with each other: they admit quite openly that they are 100% right for each other and spend hours talking and holding hands. Murakami comments, 'What a wonderful thing it is to find and be found by your 100% perfect other. It's a cosmic miracle' (lines 77 - 78). But the pair agree to go their separate ways – confident that if they are such perfect matches for each other, then they are bound to meet again in the future. The narrator ruefully comments that the test they had agreed on was 'utterly unnecessary' (line 88) and that they are so perfect together they should never have parted. In this section feelings have been presented in an idyllic way and central to what it means for human beings to be happy and fulfilled.

One winter they both catch influenza and their memories are erased. Nonetheless, they grow up and become what Murakami calls 'fully-fledged members of society' (line 99). One day, many years later, when the boy is a man of 32 and the girl is a woman of 30, they pass in the street and. although there is some glow of a memory in both of them, the adult world has changed them and they pass each other without acknowledging the other…forever.

Murakami presents feelings as absolutely central to what it means to be human and to feel happy and fulfilled. He also seems to suggest in his presentation of feelings that growing older and becoming adults affects our ability to love 100%, and this provokes a sense of loss and sadness. He says of the two young people, as they grow up, that 'they even experienced love again, sometimes as much as 75% or 85%' (lines 103 – 104), but never 100% again. In this sense, Murakami or his narrator sees the process of becoming an adult as one which diminishes our capacity to love fully and wholeheartedly, and which means we will never be able to re-capture the innocence and whole-hearted enthusiasm of our youthful feelings of total commitment and faith in the ones we choose to love.

and then part (b)

Write about how feelings are presented in **one** other story from *Sunlight on the Grass.*

In 'My Polish Teacher's Tie' the protagonist, Carla Carter, addresses the reader directly in the first person narrative. This allows us an insight into the characters innermost thoughts and feelings. The story begins with: 'I wear a uniform, blue overall and white cap with the school logo on it. Part-time catering staff, that's me, £3.89 per hour.' Instantly we get a sense of lowliness about the character, the author having chosen to reveal Carla's meagre wage and humble job at the outset, almost as if these details define her. Carla continues on line three with: 'It's not a bad job. I like the kids.' By omission the character reveals that she does not like the teaching staff and this is confirmed when she employs sarcasm to describe the teacher's tea and bun scheme:

The teachers pay for their tea and buns. It's one of those schemes teachers are good at. So much in a kitty, and that entitles them to cups of tea and buns for the rest of the term. Visitors pay, too, or it wouldn't be fair. Very keen on fairness, we are, here (line 5).

The sarcastic use of 'we' indicates a degree of resentment on the character's part. Clearly she does not perceive herself as being part of the 'we' she describes and in taking ownership of her surfaces at line 23, her sense of inadequacy or lowliness is cemented: 'I wrung out a cloth and wiped my surfaces.'

The protagonist's sense of exclusion amongst the school staff is reaffirmed at line 25 with the impenetrable collective description used to describe the teachers: 'The Head vanished in a knot of teachers...' Similarly on line 26 the character remarks: 'Teachers are used to getting out of the way of catering staff without really seeing them.' This suggests that Carla feels invisible and on line 100 the character's perceived sense of exclusion is confirmed: 'Colleagues don't wear blue overalls and white caps and work for £3.89 an hour.' She clearly does not feel part of the school's fraternity.

When Carla approaches the head he 'stitches a nice smile on his face', the use of the word 'stitching' in association with human flesh creates a painful visual image and indicates a reluctance on the Head's part to converse with the dinner lady. He then stumbles over her name at line 32: 'Oh, er – Mrs, er – Carter. Is there a problem?' This hesitancy affirms the character's sense of exclusion, the Head appears to be unfamiliar with her.

When Carla engages in letter exchanges with the Polish teacher, Steve, the writer reveals that she has possessive feelings. When Jade asks her mother about the letter on line 46, the protagonist is evasive: 'Just a letter. You can have the stamp if you want.' She responds similarly when the Head asks her whether she ever wrote to the teacher: ''Yes,' I said. Nothing more. Let him think I'd written once then not bothered....(line 76).' Both instances suggest that Carla wants to keep the correspondence private, for her eyes only.

After the story reveals that Steve is coming to England Carla's sense of inadequacy manifests again. She has failed to reveal her true role within the school and has let Steve assume that she too is teaching staff. Without this guise her feelings of worthlessness resurface: 'But what was worse was that he was going to expect to meet me. Or not me, exactly, but the person he'd been writing too, who didn't really exist (line 96).' The extent or her personal inadequacy means that despite her re-kindled love of poetry, with thoughts of Steve's rejection, she no longer feels worthy to pursue her interest (line 121): 'And then there was the poetry book I'd bought. It seemed a shame to bin it. It might come in use for Jade, I thought.' Without Steve she feels unqualified to sustain her pursuit of poetry.

When Carla finally meets Steve, Dunmore introduces metaphor and simile into Carla's words, a change which correlates with Carla's heightened emotions. The protagonist's more inventive use of language reveals a growing confidence, qualified by her connection with Steve. On line 165 the protagonist describes how Steve's song went through her 'like a knife through butter' and on line 174 she describes Steve's tie as a 'flag from another country…' The inventive imagery reveals the character's happiness and jubilation; despite her worst fears Steve has accepted her for who she is.

Note

The man's confused and mixed feelings in 'Something Old, Something New' would give you a great deal to write about in the area of feelings in his ambivalent responses to Sudan and Islamic culture. In 'When the Wasps Drowned' Eveline's feelings are often repressed or hidden, but Wigfall uses dreams to show us her horror at the discovery of the dead girl buried in the garden. In 'Compass and Torch' as well the feelings of the man and his son are expressed cleverly but indirectly through their dialogue and actions.

Printed in Great Britain
by Amazon